SMALL BUT *DEADLY*

DEADLY
POISON DART FROGS

By Lincoln James

Gareth Stevens
Publishing

Please visit our website, www.garethstevens.com. For a free color catalog of all our high-quality books, call toll free 1-800-542-2595 or fax 1-877-542-2596.

Library of Congress Cataloging-in-Publication Data

James, Lincoln.
Deadly poison dart frogs / Lincoln James.
    p. cm. — (Small but deadly)
Includes index.
ISBN 978-1-4339-5744-4 (pbk.)
ISBN 978-1-4339-5745-1 (6 pack)
ISBN 978-1-4339-5742-0 (library binding)
1. Dendrobatidae—Juvenile literature. I. Title.
QL668.E233J36 2012
597.87'7—dc22

                                        2011009417

First Edition

Published in 2012 by
Gareth Stevens Publishing
111 East 14th Street, Suite 349
New York, NY 10003

Copyright © 2012 Gareth Stevens Publishing

Designer: Michael J. Flynn
Editor: Greg Roza

Photo credits: Cover, pp. 1, (2–4, 7–8, 11–12, 15–16, 19–24 background texture), 5 (all), 6, 9, 10 (frog), 13, 14, 17, 18, 20 (frog) Shutterstock.com; p. 10 (bromeliad) iStockphoto.com; p. 18 (inset) Joe McDonald/Visuals Unlimited/Getty Images.

Printed in the United States of America

CPSIA compliance information: Batch #CS11GS: For further information contact Gareth Stevens, New York, New York at 1-800-542-2595.

CONTENTS

Words in the glossary appear in **bold** type the first time they are used in the text.

LOOK, BUT DON'T TOUCH!

Poison dart frogs—or just poison frogs—come in many bright colors. They can be yellow, blue, green, red, or orange. Many also have black shapes and spots. Scientists think there may be almost 200 **species** of poison frogs. Depending on the species, poison frogs can be 0.4 to 2.4 inches (1 to 6 cm) long.

Poison frogs look small and harmless. Most are really cute! However, as their name suggests, they're actually deadly creatures. Their skin gives off a deadly poison.

DEADLY DATA

All poison frogs are members of the scientific family Dendrobatidae. This name comes from Greek words that mean "tree walker."

These are just a few of the many different kinds of poison frogs.

Poison frogs don't need to blend into their surroundings. Their bright colors tell other animals to stay away.

IN THE JUNGLE

Poison frogs live in the rainforests of Central and South America. They're often found in great numbers. In some cases, an entire species lives in an area no bigger than 10 city blocks.

Native Americans from Colombia, South America, have long used poison frogs for hunting. They rub their **blowgun** darts on the backs of poison frogs to make poison darts. Only a small amount of poison is needed to kill a large bird or monkey quickly. That's how poison dart frogs got their name.

DEADLY DATA

Poison dart frogs are sometimes confused with mantella frogs. Mantellas are colorful, poisonous frogs from the African country of Madagascar.

LEGS AND TOES

Poison frogs are tiny. Some could even sit on your fingertip! A poison frog's back legs are larger than its front legs. This helps it jump quickly.

Unlike most frogs, poison frogs don't have **webbed** feet. Webbed feet are perfect for swimming, but most poison frogs live on land and not in water. They have three or four toes on each foot. Each toe has a sticky pad for gripping tree trunks and leaves.

DEADLY DATA

Many poison frogs like to spend most of their time in trees. In fact, some poison frogs spend their whole lives in a single tree!

This is a blue poison dart frog from South America. The local Indians call them *okopipi*.

This strawberry poison frog is carrying a tadpole on its back.

bromeliad

PIGGYBACK RIDES!

Some female poison frogs lay eggs on a leaf. The male or female watches over the eggs. When the eggs **hatch**, the tadpoles climb onto the adult's back. The adult carries the tadpoles to a tiny pool of water. This is often the water that collects in the center of a plant called a bromeliad. Some species lay eggs directly into water. Parents often watch over and feed the tadpoles. After the tadpoles grow into frogs, they crawl out of the water.

DEADLY DATA

Bromeliads, such as the pineapple, have many leaves growing out of a common base. In some bromeliads, small pools of water form where the leaves come together.

YOU ARE WHAT YOU EAT

Most poison frogs are active during the day. They hunt for tiny bugs. They mostly eat ants, beetles, and termites. Poison frogs are very good at catching bugs with their long, sticky tongues.

Many scientists think that the frogs' poison comes from the bugs they eat. The bugs' poison comes out of the frogs' skin without hurting the frogs. Poison frogs in **captivity** aren't poisonous. That's because they aren't fed the same bugs they eat in the wild.

DEADLY DATA

Poison frogs live from 5 to 12 years in zoos. No one knows how long they live in the wild.

This colorful poison frog is hunting for a meal.

Even though the blue poison dart frog is toxic, some snakes and spiders can eat it without getting hurt.

DEADLY TOXINS

A poison frog's poison is called a toxin. Toxins are poisons made by living things. The toxins come out of tiny holes in the frogs' skin. This makes the frogs unsafe for animals to touch or eat.

Many poison frog toxins are strong enough to **stun** or kill **predators**. Three are even strong enough to kill people. However, not all poison frog toxins are deadly to all animals. Some make the frogs' enemies sick. Others just taste terrible!

DEADLY DATA

Only three species of poison frogs make toxins strong enough to kill people. These are the frogs used to make poison darts.

WARNING SIGNS

Poison frogs are some of the most colorful animals in the world. However, those bright colors aren't just for looks. They keep the frogs safe. Predators see the colors and know to stay far away from these deadly little creatures. The colors tell their enemies, "I'm no good to eat!"

Some nonpoisonous frogs mimic, or copy, the bright colors of poison frogs. This is called mimicry. Mimicry keeps nonpoisonous frogs safe by making predators think they're poisonous frogs.

DEADLY DATA

The strawberry poison frog is usually red, but it can sometimes have blue legs. Some people say it looks like it's wearing blue jeans!

Stawberry poison frogs live in Nicaragua, Costa Rica, and Panama.

Unlike other poison frogs, the golden poison frog spends most of its life on the ground.

THE GOLDEN POISON FROG

The golden poison frog lives in the rainforests of Colombia. It's one of the largest poison frogs. Some grow to 2 inches (5 cm) long. Although they're called "golden" frogs, they can be yellow, orange, or green. Many have black markings, too.

The golden poison frog is one of the most poisonous animals in the world. One frog contains enough toxin to kill 10 people! It's used by the Emberá people to make deadly poison darts.

DEADLY DATA

The Amazon ground snake of Colombia eats young golden poison frogs. However, it can't eat adults because they're too poisonous!

PEOPLE AND POISON DART FROGS

Many species of poison frogs are **endangered**. Their homes are getting smaller as people cut down rainforests. Pollution also harms the frogs and their homes. It's important to keep poison frogs safe. Scientists think their toxins can be used to make new drugs, such as heart **medicines** and painkillers.

Some people keep poison frogs as pets! However, they can be hard to take care of. Only a frog **expert** should have a pet poison frog.

GOLDEN POISON FROGS UP CLOSE

scientific name	*Phyllobates terribilis* *Phyllobates* comes from the Greek words for "leaf walker" *terribilis* is Latin for "terrible" or "scary"
average length	1.85 inches (4.7 cm)
average weight	about 0.14 ounce (4 g)
food in the wild	ants, beetles, other tiny bugs
food in captivity	mostly crickets
life span	5 to 12 years in captivity

GLOSSARY

blowgun: a tube through which a dart can be shot by blowing into it

captivity: the state of being caged

endangered: in danger of dying out

expert: someone with great knowledge about a subject

hatch: to break open

medicine: a drug used to treat someone who is sick or hurt

predator: an animal that hunts other animals for food

species: a group of animals that are all of the same kind

stun: to shock something so it can't move

webbed: connected by skin

FOR MORE INFORMATION

BOOKS

Bredeson, Carmen. *Poison Dart Frogs Up Close.* Berkeley Heights, NJ: Enslow Elementary, 2009.

Ganeri, Anita. *Poison Dart Frog.* Chicago, IL: Heinemann Library, 2011.

WEBSITES

Amphibians: Poison Frog
www.sandiegozoo.org/animalbytes/t-poison_frog.html
Read about poison frogs and see pictures of them.

The Poison-Arrow Frog and the Bromeliad
rainforest-alliance.org/kids/activities/poison-frog
Learn more about poison frogs and their relationship with bromeliads.

Poison Dart Frogs
kids.nationalgeographic.com/kids/animals/creaturefeature/poison-dart-frog/
Read more about poison frogs and see pictures of them. Also watch a video of a strawberry poison frog caring for a tadpole.

Publisher's note to educators and parents: Our editors have carefully reviewed these websites to ensure that they are suitable for students. Many websites change frequently, however, and we cannot guarantee that a site's future contents will continue to meet our high standards of quality and educational value. Be advised that students should be closely supervised whenever they access the Internet.

INDEX